SECRETS TO

ONLINE

BOUTIQUE

SUCCESS

YOUR COMPREHENSIVE PLANNING GUIDE TO STARTING AND GROWING A PROFITABLE ONLINE BOUTIQUE BUSINESS

Shakeema Hughes

DEDICATION

To my lovely daughter **Nylah** who I love so much! I am hopeful to be the mother and role model that teaches you how to live a life that is filled with purpose and pleasing to God.

ACKNOWLEDGMENTS

I would first like to acknowledge God who is the head of my life. I can't do anything without God! I am truly thankful because He will keep you when you want to be kept! Even when I wasn't holding on to God's unchanging hand, He was holding on to mine, and for that I am grateful.

I would like to acknowledge my mother Ella Brown, for showing me tough love and truly instilling in me the work ethic that I carry with me today. I am appreciative that now I understand why you are a hard working woman. Because I witnessed how hard you worked it allowed me to recognize that I have to strive for my desires and do the work. Quitting is never an option! Focus and determination are the sources for my continuous desired outcome.

Special thanks to my dad Kenneth Hughes for always being a phone call away. I'm thankful that we share the same characteristics, it helps me to stay

i

strong and not to worry too much about things I have no control over.

To my family who has always supported me in every business venture I have ever had and personal victories, my grandmother Betty Smith who always instills in me to keep God first, my brothers Jesse, Rashee, Antwan, Andre, and Kenneth, sisters Vanessa who is also my assistant, Felecia, and Eboni, my god mother, aunts, uncles, cousins, nieces, nephews who believed in me and always encouraged me, you are greatly appreciated.

To my friend Capetrice Bronner who so generously blessed me with the insight I needed to open my very own boutique. If it wasn't for you I would not have known where to begin. Thank you so much, you are truly a blessing. To my friend and accountability partner Tyree Montgomery for always encouraging me and pushing me to follow my inner voice at all times, I appreciate you!

To all of my friends who always have my back at all times and inspire me to level up in every area of my life. My girls from Lincoln High School and beyond Jersey City all day, you'll already know I love you'll a bunch of lots ☺. I appreciate how real you'll are with me at all times. Your honesty and integrity does not go unnoticed.

Special thanks to Shante B, Shante G, Rochanda, Krystal, Alesha, and Tequila for always listening when I needed someone to talk to, and being there when I needed a hug and a shoulder to cry on. Life is not always easy, but I'm comforted in knowing that there are women like you, to inspire me to keep moving forward in spite of what my situations may have looked like at the time.

To my friend and sister in Christ Natalie, you are truly heaven sent. I thank God for allowing us to meet and be a part of this life. It is because of you that I have become part of an amazing church home but more importantly, I have a new found relationship with my creator. I thank you for always leading by example, being honest at all times even when it hurts, and encouraging me to know the word of God for myself, teaching me, and guiding me to follow God no matter what it may cost me!!

To my coach Nicole Cooper, who encouraged me to share this information with the world. It was because of your coaching program that *Open An Online Boutique* was established. Your insight and knowledge of this industry motivated me to get started immediately. I decreed and declared that 2015 was the year of implementation. The coaching sessions along with implementation of the plan for 2014 allowed this is all to happen. Thank you so much.

To Tiana Von Johnson who is one of the best branding coaching and business building strategist I know, I thank you for your coaching and commitment to my brand. Your skillset, knowledge, and experience with building a business and branding is unbelievable. I recognize and continue to show gratitude to you for having patience with me because a lot of it I didn't understand at first. My mindset was not at the level it is on today and I truly want to thank you for that. The exposure and opportunities that you provided me allowed me to think outside the box. It made me step all the way out of my comfort zone, allowed me to see that I can do and have all of the things I wanted and more. Working with you has not only benefited my life professionally, but it has also increased my life on a personal level as well. Thank you. Thank you. Thank you!

To all of the men and women who support my business ventures, and sent emails with your stories, you are the reason why I wrote this book. It inspired me to keep going, to keep sharing, and to keep building others up. I pray this book helps you to realize the importance of entrepreneurship and how to leverage the internet to create wealth for you and your family.

CONTENTS

INTRODUCTION

Congratulations! You have made a decision to continue to perfect your craft and learn everything you need to know about opening and maintaining your online business! Opening a boutique whether it is online or offline can be scary, especially if you don't have any experience. You may be thinking to yourself, "All I have to do is post pictures on Instagram and people will see it and buy my products!" While that may be fantastic, that's not reality. Most online boutiques that post pictures on Instagram are just leveraging a platform for the business owner to bring more awareness to their boutique. Others are just "doing it for the Gram" but are not making any money.

I am not trying to scare you or talk you out of opening your very own boutique, but I do want you to know that if this is something you truly want to do you must be consistent and persistent. There may be times when you want to give up, but you have to always keep it in your mind the reason for opening your online boutique. Once you allow your faith to be bigger than your fears you will succeed!

I am an entrepreneur at heart so starting my very own online boutique was an idea that I felt could work. I liked some of the styles that were out, but most of the clothing was a little too reveling for me. I wanted to start a clothing line for classy, sophisticated workingwomen with a little bit of an edge. All of my friends share the same style so I figured there was a market for me to tap in to.

My journey started by searching for wholesale manufactures that carried the style of clothing I was looking for, but I began to get frustrated. As I searched the Internet I found that many stores use the word "wholesale" in their name but they are far from wholesale providers. Many of them were scam artist looking for ways to rip people off and take their hard earned money.

I work two jobs, go to school, and I am a single mother of a beautiful daughter, and I refuse to be ripped off by people or organizations that seek to take advantage of people who want to make an honestly living, but lacking the knowledge needed to find the right information. I looked, and search, and researched some more to find quality wholesale providers for my up and coming boutique, but I found nothing.

The year was starting to come to an end. I was upset because I wanted to go into the New Year with my online boutique. I was discouraged and after a while I was done with the entire idea. Then I noticed a network marketing company that I was affiliated with having a conference in Miami, FL. At first I wasn't going to attend because any one that know me knows that I do not like to fly. The other reason I didn't want to attend was because I would have to go alone. I didn't have anyone that was as serious about personal and professional development as I am to partner up with in my area so it left me to do a lot of things by myself. I prayed about it and said, *"God, if it's for me to go on this trip please provide a way. If not, I know it's not for me. Reveal to me what it is that I am supposed to do to generate an income that will allow me to provide for my daughter and myself, and pay off my debt. In Jesus name, Amen."*

A few days went by and I started to feel like this trip was not going to happen. I didn't get a sign from God or anything. On my way home from work I started to brainstorm about the next big thing I would do and be a part of. Once I made it home I was rushing to get in the door to get a pen and my journal so that I can write everything down that came to my head. I saw that I had mail so I figured I'd grab it before I went inside. Once I got in the house I threw the mail on the table, grab my pen and journal, and

3

wrote down everything I could think of for my next big thing. I looked across the table and looked at the stack of mail and thought to myself, maybe I should open those to see what bills I need to pay.

As I was going through the mail I saw an envelope I wasn't familiar with. I opened it and started to read it slowly. When I realized that it was money I started to thank God immediately! I made sure everything was legit because I felt myself getting way too excited! Once I realized that all was well, I proceeded to book my flight and hotel for Miami!

I knew that this trip was heaven sent. I knew it was something that I needed to get from going on this trip. I knew that going on this trip was going to change my life for the better. I knew that this trip was going to provide the answers to a lot of questions. I knew that I was going to be forced to get out of my comfort zone. I knew that this trip wasn't going to be business as usual. I knew that this trip was going to force me to be the person I should have been years ago. I knew it was time for a change, and I was ready!

Scared, nervous, and every other emotion was slowing taking over my body as I waited to board this plane to Miami. I started to second-guess this trip but then I had to check myself. I had to tell myself that if this trip wasn't what God wanted He would not have made it happen. I had to remind myself that all of these questions would be answered, and a shift was going to take place in me as a result of going on this trip.

I slowly started to relax and I just said a prayer. After I said Amen, it was time to board the plane. I put my game face on, boarded that plane, positioned myself comfortably in my seat, closed my eyes, and before I knew it the plane was taking off. When I opened my eyes good, the flight attendant was saying, Welcome to Miami!

Fresh off of a flight from New Jersey to Miami and I'm feeling great! It's about eighty degrees and I love the Florida sunshine. I rented a vehicle and proceeded down 95 South straight to the conference, which was starting in a half an hour. I made it just in time to get a seat close to the stage.

While I found that I learned a lot of information I didn't know before, I still felt that I needed more. I took ample notes from each and every speaker that was there. I started to get restless because I'd been up since 4:00am and didn't get any rest beside the catnap on the plane. I was going to go to my hotel room but I overheard a few people talking about the mix and mingle that was going on right after the conference so I decided to stay and mingle.

I was one of the first to arrive at the mix and mingle, almost like a second wind, the excitement came over me even though I hadn't slept in over 16 hours. Music was playing and drinks were being served so I decided to get me a glass of ginger ale. I went over to one of the tables and just hung out there. I was enjoying the music but then I started to feel drained because I didn't get enough rest. I noticed more people coming into the party so I decided I would stay a little while longer. Three women walked in about 5 minutes apart and they all kind of gravitated toward my table. They introduced themselves one by one and then we all just started talking. We all exchanged numbers so that we can sit next to each other at the conference tomorrow. After we exchanged numbers we all called it a night.

The next day we texted each other and we met up in a central location to go to the conference. When it was time to break for lunch we all walked to the Subway Restaurant to get sandwiches. We all told stories about how we found out about the company's conference and why we decided to partner with them. The conversation was interesting but it got even more interesting when we started sharing what it is we do for a living. One of the ladies worked a 9-5 for a private owned business. Another woman was a pharmacist looking to get into entrepreneurship, which is what drew her to attend the conference. The other young lady was an entrepreneur. I asked her what type of business she owned and informed her that I am an entrepreneur as well. She told me she owned her own online business. I said, "Doing what?" She said, "Selling women's clothing"! When she said that my face lit up! I knew at that very moment she was the woman I was supposed to meet to get the information I had been searching for, for months now. Unfortunately for me it was time for us to head back to the conference so I couldn't ask her as many questions as I wanted to, but I knew that time was coming.

After the conference the ladies and myself went to a private coaching session with a mentor that we all shared. We ended up staying in our coach's hotel room talking until 2:00 in the morning. I had to be back at my hotel, pack, and at the airport in 3 hours. Once I realized I would not get to talk to the young lady I met who owned her own boutique, I was upset. I just kept saying to myself in the car driving back to my hotel, how I got this close to the information I needed and leave without it. I just couldn't seem to understand that. I was so drained from the long day that we had, I just packed my bags, drove to the airport, got on the plane and went back home, filled with disappointment, and like I wasted my time and money.

One week went by and I remember my coach saying she was going to have a private event in Miami in February. I reached out to all of the ladies I met at the conference and ask them if they heard any information about the private event taking place next month. The lady who owned her own boutique said she did and was going to attend. I sent her a private message letting her know I wanted to talk to her because I was very interested in her business model and wanted to know more about it. She was very much open to the idea and couldn't wait to chat. That gave me hope because coming back from Miami I felt like I took 3 steps backwards instead of forward. I didn't get my hopes up; I just went with the flow.

Once we all received our invites to the private event from my coach, all of the ladies decided it would be a great idea if we all stayed in a room together. The boutique owner who is also a travel agent got us some great rates on hotel rooms and suites at some of the finest hotels in South Beach. We all put our money together and book the hotel and flights for the trip. I was determined that on this trip, I was not leaving until she gives me at least some type of website that will help me to find wholesale providers.

I'm back in Miami after just being here one-month ago and I must say it felt great! In New Jersey it's cold and it snowed every weekend so to be in eighty degree weather, see people walking on south beach with bathing suits on, and being able to walk right out the back door of the hotel and walk along the beach made me feel like I was in paradise. I was feeling great, but I had to come back down to reality. I knew I was in Miami for a mission, and I couldn't leave until the mission was accomplished.

Once all of the ladies where at the hotel we decided to go for a walk on the beach to catch up and hear everyone purpose for coming, and what they wanted to take away from this trip. We all made a sacrifice to be there so we wanted to get the most out of it. After hearing everyone's reason for coming back to Miami one month later it was clear to me why we all connected in the way that we did. We came back to Miami because we needed answers to our direct questions. We came back to Miami because we realize that an important piece to our life puzzle was missing and we needed to find it to make everything complete. We came to Miami a month later because we knew that if we didn't we would be stuck in the same place we are in now, feeling incomplete, lost, unfulfilled, hopeless, wanting to abort our future, and feeling like we are not capable of completing the mission that we thought was divine. Some spent their rent money, some left their children with spouse's who didn't approve of going on this trip, but they went anyway. Some knew that when they went back home they wouldn't have a job because their time wasn't approved by their boss, but came to Miami anyway. Other's maxed out credit cards to go back to Miami because they felt they would find that missing puzzle piece needed to make everything complete. Being in an intimate setting with women who have made 7 figures in a little over a year who were going to give us the blueprint to create wealth for our families and ourselves was the reason why we came on this trip. The conference last month was cool, but we all needed that face-to-face, straight talk, real and raw interaction with these 7 figure earners so that we can be clear on what we are doing wrong, and what we need to start doing immediately to make things right.

After meeting with the 7 figure earners and having a chance to build that relationship with them the ladies and myself agreed that the trip was so worth it! I learned more about making money, building an empire, and building relationships with people from this trip then I learned going to college and yes I am a college graduate. The information that was poured into us on this trip people would normally pay five, even ten thousand dollars for this type of information at a seminar. We were so excited about the knowledge we all went back to our room to write down our action plans, and things we were going to implement when we all got back home.

One by one we shared our plans. After everyone went I asked the young lady that owned the boutique about her business plan and how she went about doing it. Before the trip I told myself I was not leaving without some type of information about starting a boutique and I was determined to get what I needed. At first she shared with me her reasons for wanting to open a boutique. I went on to ask her how she found out about wholesale providers. I shared with her my journey in researching this information and how discouraged I was in the process. Wouldn't you know our stories were similar? She told me how difficult it was for her to find the wholesale providers as well. She did her Internet search and failed. She went as far as calling other boutique owners and asking for their wholesale provider, but they wouldn't share their sources with her. The great thing about this woman was that she was ambitious. She did not let that stop her. She went on to ordering products from this boutique owner, looking at the boxes the items came in, and the tags on the inside to find out who the manufacturer was for that particular item and called them. She also continued to call other boutique owners as well.

It was one boutique owner that she ordered a garment from and she decided to give the owner a call. She started off by thanking the owner of the boutique for getting her garment to her as fast as she did. She went on to tell the owner that she is an aspiring boutique owner and wanted to know the name of the wholesale provider the boutique owner does business with. The boutique owner was a little skeptical, but after the woman shared her story with the owner of the boutique, and gave her a name of a wholesale provider she was going to do business with but wasn't sure and needed help, the owner begin to open up to her. By the end of the conversation this boutique owner ended up giving her the wholesale providers she did business with, how she can go about setting up her accounts with them, and some of the manufacturers she personally works with. I said wow, that's amazing! The young lady was like I know I was amazed as well. But just like me she was determined to not give up. She ended up going online and showing me as well as the other women the wholesale provider that she does business with, and gave us all the information we needed to open our own boutiques as well. She even took us to the wholesale district in Miami so we can see some of the items and allow us to build relationships with some of the owners.

Her willingness and dedication to helping people and wanting to see others win inspired me to write this book. I decided to write this book because I want to give you the tools and tips you need to not just open, but maintain an online boutique. You see my good friend I met in Miami gave me the tools I needed to get started, and I am very grateful. But what I do know is that there is so much more you need to know before you open your very own online boutique and I want to share it with you.

After reading this book you will know the common mistakes that new boutique owners make, you will have your M.A.P. and the Open and Maintain an Online Boutique Principles you must follow. With these tools you will not only be able to open a successful online boutique, but you will be able to maintain it as well. Let get into the details shall we!!

LEVEL 1

FOUNDATION

Chapter 1

WHY YOU NEED TO LIVE THIS HERE LIFSTYLE

Growing up I always knew that I wanted to have a business that I could call my own. I always had dreams of working for myself, and being able to make my own money without anyone dictating how much money I could make. I know that I am not the only one who has that burning desire to be an entrepreneur! I know that there are some ups and downs but I was determined to jump into it and find out through trial and error how things work.

When I was in high school some of my friends and I put together this bus ride to Great Adventure. We knew that it was a group rate when there are over 10 people attending. My friends and I determined what the group rate was, found out how much the bus would cost to take us there and back, and charged them accordingly so that the three of us can split the profits. Once the transaction was done and I split the money with my friends, all types of things started running through my mind. That moment ignited a fire in me! I knew that was a moment I wanted to have for the rest of my life, and ever since then I have created ways to make that happen.

After graduating high school I went directly to a community college in my area and decided to major in business since owning a business was part of my plan. I worked at a local supermarket to keep money in my pocket, but truth be told the money just wasn't enough. I ended up landing a job at a bank which sent my self-esteem through the roof only to get treated unfairly, be miserable, angry, and get disrespected on the regular.

My intentions for my new bank job was to learn how to manage my personal finances, my business finances once I opened my own business, and what programs the bank offered to help small business owners. I was excited about this new chapter in my life because it was a new level for me. No more working with high school students, but now I'm in the big leagues so I thought! Working for the bank was an eye opening experience for me, one that I hope no one ever has to go through.

Of course, everything starts off good. I'm getting along with my coworkers; I'm learning new things, and the customers like me which is a big deal when you are working in the customers' service field. Then things started to go left, way left. I found out I was pregnant which wasn't a problem for me, but that's when it seemed like all of the problems started. There would be some days I didn't move as fast as I use to because my body was changing and I was having a hard time adjusting to the new change. My supervisor was very understanding, but my manager on the other hand was not.

He started questioning my personal life, which was very uncomfortable to me. He use to ask about my relationship with my daughter's father and if we planned on getting married. Now to me that's none of his business, but then I thought maybe he just wanted the best for me so I proceeded to entertain him. His response to my answers started to become very offensive. For example, I told him how old I was which at the time I was 19. He would say things like, "you are way too young to be having a baby what were you thinking". I would look at him asking myself, why is he talking to me like this. I know I needed to keep my job because in a few months I would be having a baby, so I shut my mouth and continued to perform my job duties.

As head teller my job consisted of lifting heavy coins, counting money, and opening and closing the vault, which by the way is a very heavy door. During this time I made my supervisor, as well as the customer service representative know that this is not something I could continue to do once I had gotten further along in my pregnancy. They understood and would help me during that time, but one day it seemed like it came to a halt. To my surprise, they were told by the manager to no longer assist me because those duties were a part of my job description, and it needed to be taken care of by me alone. Let's be clear, I was not asking them to perform my job duties. I was asking them to carry heavy coins and open the vault door for me, nothing more, and nothing less.

About seven months into my pregnancy things started to get more difficult for me. My ankles began to swell daily and my energy levels were at an all-time low. I decided to have a meeting with my manager because I would be going on maternity leave sooner than later and wanted to make sure things would be ok, and get the tellers organized while I was gone. I'm thinking this is a great idea, and shows much leadership qualities, but clearly I was wrong. I went into the meeting with a plan and a way for things to continue while I was gone. He came into the meeting with a list of things I never do, didn't do right, or failed in as the head teller. I was shocked because I would have thought if things were not going well, he as the manager would have scheduled a meeting a long time ago to inform me, and make plans so that I could right my wrongs. Instead he dropped this bomb on me when physically and emotionally I was at my lowest.

He said mean things to me like, "you are one of the

worst tellers I ever hired". He also use to say things like, you are so ridiculous. But it was one thing he said to me that made me look at life differently which was, I don't even know why I still ALLOW you to work here. When he said these words to me, my whole life flashed before my eyes.

First of all, if I am a horrible teller how am I able to assist my teller line, resolve any teller related issue, win every contest, and be number one in quality customer service? If I am that ridiculous, why is it that every bank operation is done completely, and we pass every audit. If you question why you still allow me to work here, why didn't you fire me a long time ago? And yes I asked him these questions because I wanted answers. I was very offended by the things he said to me.

My take on the entire meeting was, how dare you! How dare you insult me! How dare you insult my intelligence! How dare you sit here and try to belittle me and my ambition! How dare you threaten me by insinuating you are going to fire me while I am 7 months pregnant! How dare you! It was in that moment that I knew I needed something different. Something I could call my own. It was in that moment I knew I had to continue on my journey to opening my very own business. It was in that moment I knew I had to rise above this situation and focus on what was important. It was in that moment I knew that I could not let anyone dictate my income and threaten to take my lively hood.

I went home after that meeting and was filled with anger. I could not stop crying. I could not stop replaying what happened in the meeting. I could not understand why all of this was happening to me. It was in my replay of the events, I remembered what my intentions were for this job. My intention was to learn how to manage my personal finances. I did that! My intention was to learn about business finance in regard to startup cost. I did that! My intention was to find out what programs were available for small business owners. I did that too!

It was in that moment, I realized that for a short while I lost sight of my vision. I realized that if I did not go through that experience I would not have the ambition needed to continue. That terrible experience is what re-lit my fire. That experience was the fuel that I needed to continue my pursuit of business ownership.

I took a negative experience and turned it into a positive mission and you should too. I know that you have your own horror story and it's ok. Don't let it cripple you. Instead use it to catapult your life in a direction that will allow you to reap the benefits personally and professionally.

Owning your very own business comes with many benefits. It isn't just about being the boss which by the way isn't a bad thing. So many people have a negative connotation about the word boss. I can understand because it is a word that can be overly used and exaggerated. The truth is, YOU ARE A BOSS! You are the boss of your life. You are the boss of your finances; you are the boss of your home. You are the boss of your body. You are the boss of your decisions. Now it is time for you to make the necessary moves by becoming a business owner.

Being a business owner is about freedom, choices, desire, and convenience. There are so many reasons why you need to live this here lifestyle. I want to share with you 6 reasons why you should become an online business owner.

1. **Generate an income from something you are passionate about**: There is nothing more fulfilling then doing something you enjoy. Whether you are selling clothes, shoes, offering a service, training products, pet accessories, or hair products, your passion for this will allow you to generate an income that will allow you to take care of yourself and your family. When you have a desire and you are passionate about something, it doesn't feel like a job. You can actually get up in the morning and be excited about your business knowing that you are providing a product or a service that is helping someone in need while generating an income for you and your family.

2. **Make your own decisions.** Becoming a business owner allows you to make your own decisions. No one can dictate to you what to do, when to do it, and how much money they are going to pay you to do it. You dictate how much you want to make. You have creative control over your business. You are the boss of your business.

3. **Run your business your way.** In becoming a business owner you can operate in your own timing and do things that are convenient for you. For example, you can schedule a time to call your customers during evening hours. This way you can work your job during the day, spend time with the children when you get home, and make time for your business by returning emails and phone calls for an hour in the evening.

4. **Freedom!** The ultimate goal when opening a business is to have time freedom. Freedom to eat lunch when you want. Freedom to vacation when you want. Freedom to determine how much you are worth. Freedom to drop your children off and pick them up from school. Financial freedom! Freedom to enjoy this thing called life.

5. **Showcase your products or services to the world**. When you are in business and you only have a store front, you're limited to the amount of customers that will come into your store to make a purchase. If you took this same business and made it available to people online, you could

attract more customers.   With the internet you would be able to sell your products or services to people across the world who love the products you have to offer.

6. **You can operate your business from any location**: If you lead a busy life like I do you have to have a business that you can operate on the go. Having an online boutique is one of those businesses that you can run while you're doing laundry, taking a lunch break, or while waiting for the bread to pop up out of the toaster! Using a smart phone or a tablet you can write emails to customers, check your inventory, and post on social media anything pertaining to your boutique business!

Boutique Reflections

After reading this chapter, what were your aha moments?

_____

_____

_____

_____

_____

_____

_____

_____

_____

_____

_____

_____

_____

_____

_____

_____

_____

_____

Chapter 2

ONLINE BOUTIQUE MISCONCEPTIONS

There is such a misconception about boutiques and the products they offer. When most people think about a boutique they think that it is a store that sells overpriced clothing that not many people can afford. While you do have some boutique's that sell garments of high quality for a large amount, not all boutiques are the same. Just so that we have a better understanding of what a boutique is, I decided to look up the definition. The definition of boutique according to Merriam Webster Dictionary is, "a small company that offers highly specialized services or products". So you see, boutiques don't necessarily have to provide products, it can also provide a service. A list of products or services that a boutique can provide is as follow:

1. Women's clothing
2. Men's clothing
3. Children's clothing
4. Shoes
5. Accessories
6. Women's body shaping garments
7. Photography services
8. Law services
9. Hair care products
10. Branding services
11. Marketing services
12. Health and wellness products
13. Personal growth products
14. Financial management services
15. Cosmetic products

These are just a few of the products and services online boutiques can offer. Don't limit yourself by believing that an online boutique can only sell clothes. We all have something that makes us unique. Even if you know someone that is selling makeup that doesn't mean they are going to brand, market, and distribute their cosmetic line like you will. Take a look at this list, find what it is you are passionate about, and move forward with creating a boutique that will allow you to follow your passion and generate an extra income. The sky is not the limit, your belief system is!

Another misconception about boutiques is that you can never make a lot of money. What exactly is a lot of money? I ask this question because I want you to think about it. What is a lot of money to you? Is that amount of money a lot to someone else? My thing is this; everyone's definition about money is different. A lot of money to you may be $1 million dollars. To someone else $1 million dollars is nothing. You have to determine how much of a profit you would like to make from your business. Calculate how much money that would be yearly. Then break it down into a monthly goal, weekly goals, and daily goals. Slow and steady always wins the race. Don't get caught up in other people's experience and he say she say. Set your income goal and make it happen!

Do you believe that being a sales person is what you need to run a profitable boutique business? Ill answer that question for you, NO! You do not need to be a sales professional to run an online boutique business. I hear people say all the time, I don't like selling. Let me share something with you. If you offer a product or a service that you know for sure people need you are going to share that information with them. Isn't that correct? If you knew I was in need of a hair stylist and know of a great hair stylist that is reasonably priced and does an amazing job, would you tell me? Of course you would. That is all you are doing. You are sharing information with the people you know need help in that area. It's not selling when you know it's something they need. We will talk more about this later in the book.

Boutique Notes

After reading this chapter, what were your aha moments?

_____

_____

_____

_____

_____

_____

_____

_____

_____

_____

_____

_____

_____

_____

_____

_____

_____

_____

_____

_____

_____

_____

_____

_____

_____

_____

_____

Chapter 3

ONLINE BOUTIQUE STATE OF MIND

Owning a boutique is an exciting experience, but you must remember that you are running a business. When you are running a business there is a certain mindset you must have or you will lose sight of your goals and the things that you set out to accomplish. If you don't have a specific mindset when it comes to your boutique you are guaranteed to fail.

When I first opened my very own business I partnered with a woman I knew was seasoned in the hair industry, but was an amateur when it came to running her own business. We were both at the salon one evening filled with customers waiting to be serviced. We noticed a pattern with the customers. Each and every one of them wanted us to recommend a product they could use while they were maintaining their hairstyle at home. As a hairstylist you recommend products to your customers all the time. This particular day after we were all done with the customers and was cleaning up the salon we both said out loud that we need to get products to sell in the salon. The amount of customers asking us to recommend products to them let us know that there was a demand. The demand from my prospective was that customers wanted to get all of their hair needs from one place. From the seasoned stylist prospective it was an additional stream of income that we could each make from the customers. We thought it was a great idea and proceeded to move forward with getting the products.

My mindset about having products in the salon was to not just sell them to our current customers, but to also sell them to the public. If we operated on this level we would have to be open the hours of other beauty supply stores in the area. The seasoned stylist agreed and that is what we did.

Once the store was open and it was time to schedule hours and perform like a traditional beauty supply store business, things went left. In the beginning it seemed we both had the same mindset in regard to the business, but as time went on I realized that our mindset was totally different. Her mindset was to operate during salon hours; my mindset was to operate during salon hours as well as traditional beauty supply store hours, which would cause us to be open a little later. Her mindset was that we should just offer the products to our current customers, which at the time wasn't consistent because we were just beginning. My mindset was if we are not going to operate as a traditional beauty supply store business and a beauty salon to attract more customers, I didn't think we should move forward with the plan.

I share this with you because I want you to realize that everyone involved has to have the same mindset. Even if you are starting this business on your own and you are the only decision maker, if you don't have a specific mindset and traits of a business owner, the business will be in jeopardy. I want to share with you a mindset that will guarantee your boutique to fail:

1. **Working when you feel like it**: You can't open your boutique and work when you feel like it. This is a guaranteed way to fail. You have to expect long hours in the beginning until you set up a plan that will compliment your schedule and allow you to be a success in your business.

2. **Get rich quick**: Opening a boutique is not a get rich quick scheme. While you can make a significant amount of money opening your own boutique, you must know that everything happens in its own timing and not all at once. Proper planning, marketing, along with other principles,

which we will discuss later in this book, can get you there. This is not a get rich quick business so if that is what you are in it for, you shouldn't even bother.

3. **I don't need a plan for my business**: In everything that you do, you need a plan. It doesn't have to be too fancy. Simply write down the vision you have for your boutique. What makes it different? What are the strengths, weakness, threats, and opportunities that your business has? Start by answering these questions. It is essential that you have a plan for your business and operate on the principles I will discuss shortly.

4. **Online businesses do not require a boss to oversee them:** If you have this mindset you are sure to fail in your business. It doesn't matter if your business is online or offline, if you are the owner of this business you are the boss! You have to oversee your business. You have to set goals, plan, and work your business just as you would for a job where someone else is paying you do to the work.

If you don't already have a boutique state of mind you need to adapt it immediately. It is only when you have a boutique state of mind you will do what is required to not just open, but grow your online boutique. Some of the character traits you want to have are as follow:

1. **Positive attitude** – having a positive attitude is very important. You can have a beautiful online boutique offering some of the best products or services, but if your attitude is constantly negative and you have bad energy no one is going to do business with you.

2. **Self-starter** – you have to be in a place where if no one else sees your vision you are going to move forward with making it happen anyway. Don't get discouraged when you share your plans and goals with people and they don't respond the way you want them to. Use that as fuel to get started. Show them by implementing your plans. Learn to get started without anyone having to pump you up, or waiting for someone to tell you it's ok for you to start. Start now!

3. **Open minded** – Keep an open mind when it comes to your online business. Have your own style of course, but take some time to see what's new and exciting in the industry that you are a part of. If customers are responding to it in a positive way figure out how to add it to your collection. Don't be so quick to turn it down. See how you can add products or services to your business and put your own spin on it.

4. **Good listening skills** – the way to keeping customers is to listen to them. If you don't listen to your customers and continue to operate the way you want, you will be out of business soon. Listen

to your customers and try to implement things that will allow you to keep customers satisfied.

5. **Financial discipline** – Allow a budget to be your best friend. A budget allows you to track every area of your finances. Start with a personal budget. See how you do with that. Make the necessary changes to move forward in a positive direction. When it is time to start a business budget you will already have the discipline you need to move forward confidently.

In addition to the character traits listed above, having these qualities will be sure to assist you in having the mindset you need to operate a successful boutique business.

- Integrity
- Ambition
- Enthusiasm
- Intuition
- Honesty
- Creativity
- Leadership skills
- Organization

Boutique Notes

After reading this chapter, what were your aha moments?

_____
_____
_____
_____
_____
_____
_____
_____
_____
_____
_____
_____
_____
_____
_____
_____
_____
_____
_____
_____
_____
_____
_____
_____
_____
_____
_____

Chapter 4

COMMON MISTAKES ONLINE BOUTIQUE OWNERS MAKE

When I decided I wanted to be my own boss and own a boutique, so many things started running through my mind. I started to think of all of the other businesses that I had in the past. I started thinking about how those businesses got started and why they are closed today. I started thinking about marketing and branding with the last business I owned and wondered if I did things the right way. It's safe to say all of the negative things came to my mind before opening my boutique.

There were some good things however, that came to my mind as well. One thing that came to mind was the liberty to set prices that would be affordable to my potential customers. Thinking of things that would help my customers to be the best and look their best brought joy to my heart, and put some excitement in my life! Don't misunderstand me, there are going to be things that happen in your business that you will not be excited about. You may run out of products that customers have paid for which forces them to have to wait or request their money back. You may forget to ship out someone's order because you were overwhelmed. You may even forget to set up a marketing campaign and think you have it all together, and forget to create the funnel so that your potential customers can actually purchase your product. All of these things happened to me so I understand and know first-hand what this feels like. My job is to try and get you to cut down on the mistakes you will make in your business. While there are many mistakes that can be made, I've listed four of the most common mistakes boutique owners make:

MISTAKE #1: CHOOSING A MARKET THAT IS OVER CROWDED

When deciding on a market to choose from when opening your boutique, you want to make sure that the market is not over crowded. To give you an example I want to use the hair industry. I am a licensed hair stylist so I follow many other hair stylists and I see that a lot of them are getting into selling hair. I'm going to be honest with you'll, selling hair is an industry that is overwhelming crowded and competitive. Everyone is selling hair! When it's time to promote your hair you will be in competition with these same hair stylists. You will have problems standing out from the rest of them, you will have to sell you hair at a ridiculously low amount to gain customers, and you probably won't get any traffic in marketing online. What you can decide to do is offer shampoo and conditioner, styling gel, or holding spray. If you are a hair braider you can offer an anti-itch spray, or something to that affect. Choose your market wisely. If it is an overcrowded market, come up with ways that will allow your business to stand out.

MISTAKE #2: LOOKING FOR WHOLESALE PROVIDERS ONLINE

I'm going to be honest with you'll and say you will NOT find any good wholesale providers online! I say this because I have experienced this for myself and it almost put me in a place where I didn't want to follow my dreams of owning my own boutique. Every wholesale provider that I have access to I had to pay for it. There was only one person that blessed me with giving me one wholesale provider for free and I thank her every time I see her because she didn't have to. Good quality wholesale providers don't market online because they don't want to be overwhelmed with calls from mom and pop stores asking questions about their products. This is why I took the time to create a list of quality wholesale providers for you. I don't want you to think you can just do a Google search and they all will appear on the first and second pages because they are not! To get access to my list of wholesale providers for clothing, shoes, accessories, body shapers, health and wellness products, electronics, and more, go to openanonlineboutique.com/oaob-wholesale-directory

MISTAKE #3: YOU HAVE NO DAILY MARKETING ROUTINE

If you do not have a daily marketing routine to market your boutique you mine as well not even bother. You can have great products, services, and more, but if no one knows you are open for business how do you think you are going to make an income? It's not possible! Get a marketing plan together immediately. Then break down your plan into daily activities that will get you the results you want in your business. Marketing is essential to your business. I have a plan that will help you to market your boutique effectively. I will discuss it later in this book.

MISTAKE #4: NOT HAVING A UNIQUE VALUE PROPOSITION

What makes you stand out from the rest of the boutique owners that sell the very same things you sell? Even if your products are not all the same but they are similar, what makes you unique? Many boutique owners go wrong in this area because they are too busy blending in with everyone and not standing out. Do yourself a favor, look in the mirror and ask yourself what make you different from all of the rest. Write those things down. Use that list to come up with your unique value proposition and use it when marketing your boutique.

To lessen your mistakes as an aspiring or emerging boutique owner, it will be wise of you to continue educating yourself in the industry you are a part of. I mentioned earlier that I am a licensed cosmetologist. I went to every hair show and attended classes that were related to hair and makeup. I brought DVDS, CDS, and collaborated with other stylist in the area to bring expose to my business. You have to be in the know about your industry. Continually educating yourself is the key to making fewer mistakes in your business.

Another great way to lessen your chances of making many mistakes is to seek wise counsel. I was able to get the information I needed to open a clothing boutique because I spoke with a young lady I met who already had experience in this area. She was very helpful in giving me the information I needed to get started. If you know a person who is doing something similar to what you are trying to do with you boutique, talk to them about it. Having candid conversation about business and what it takes to run it properly will be a tremendous start.

It will also be beneficial for you to get a mentor or business coach. If you don't know anyone who is willing to take the time and help you with your business for free, getting a mentor or business coach is necessary. If it wasn't for my business coach I would not be where I am today. My business coach is experienced in her field and knows her stuff. The resources she has given me to get my business up and running were priceless. The personal attention that she has given me and my business is incredible. The conversations that we have stretch my mind to think bigger when it comes to my business and my brand as a whole.

Things like this don't normally come for free. If it does, it's because that person helping you has positioned themselves to reap a financial benefit from your success. Don't have a cheap state of mind when it comes to your business. Train your mind to see it as making an investment in your business. An investment guarantees a return. Make the investment needed to gain the knowledge necessary to take your business to another level. Remember, its levels to this!

Boutique Notes

After reading this chapter, what were your aha moments?

_____

_____

_____

_____

_____

_____

_____

_____

_____

_____

_____

_____

_____

_____

_____

_____

_____

_____

LEVEL 2

PREP TIME

Chapter 5

ONLINE BOUTIQUE INSPIRATION

What is it that inspires you? Close your eyes and think about it. Did you get a visual? Does that visual connect with your purpose? Without having a purpose and a vision for your boutique it will not last long. You must have your vision written down so that you will have something to reference when moving forward with your business plan.

The biggest question I get in my inbox is how do I get started. When I get this question from potential boutique owners I always have a follow up question for them and that is, why do you want to open an online business and what is your plan for your boutique? When I ask these questions many people pause, for a really long time. Some email me or if we are face to face they will look at me and say, *I don't have a plan for my boutique!*

The most important step when deciding to open any business is to have a plan. Write down what your vision is for your boutique. Is this a short-term project or a long term project? Do you want to provide a product or a service? If you are providing a product to your potential customers are you creating it or are you promoting an already made product? These are just a few of the questions that need to be answered before you open a business.

If you already have your online boutique and have been in business for a while, it's never too late to re-establish your vision for your boutique. By re-establishing your vision and plan for your boutique you will be able to find your ideal customers, and you can consider offering additional products or services to them.

Write your vision and make it plain (Habakkuk 2:2). What is your vision when it comes to your boutique and how you want it to run? Write down all of the ideas that you have about the type of business you want to start.

Where there is no vision, people perish (Proverb 29:18)

Perish—to die or be killed: to disappear or be destroyed: to cease to exist: to slowly break apart by a natural process. Do you want your dreams of opening an online boutique to perish? Be diligent in making sure your vision for your online boutique is viable. If you have to, make a vision board. Place *Post It* everywhere around your home or office. Do whatever it takes! Do what is necessary to follow your dreams of opening an online boutique and bring it to life!

Do not conform to the pattern of this world, but be transformed by the renewing of your mind... (Romans 12:2). Don't do this just because it will make you some quick money. Do this because you are passionate about it! Do it because it's your desire. Do it because it's something you want to share with the world and this is the way you are going about doing it. If you only do this because you see everyone else do it, it will not last long and you will be upset with yourself!

Get yourself a journal so you can write down your activity so that you will be able to go back and reference it daily. Use your journal to be able to track your progress and your results.

Listed below are a few things I want you to **pay close attention to**. You want to immediately identify these things when and if it happens because it will be harmful to you and your business.   This infection is called failure.   Listed below are a few reasons why people fail:

1. They don't know who they are
2. They try to be like everyone else except themselves
3. They have no confidence in themselves

4. They are fearful and fear what people will say about the things they are doing
5. They have no interest in what it is that they are doing, they are just doing it for the benefits or the money

When you have your vision in front of you and you believe it can become a reality it will!! You have to first:

- Visualize it
- Document it
- Map it out
- Create the steps to make it happen
- Make your quarterly, monthly, weekly, and daily goals.
- Take action

I want you to have your own brain storming session. In this session I want you to do the following:

- Spend some time thinking over your ideas.
- Decide on the goals and vision that matter the most to you for your boutique. Write them down and read it three times a day.
- Is this a short-term project or a long-term project? Write the answer along with the reason for your answer.
- Determine if you want to provide a product or a service?
- What is the product or service that you will offer your potential customers?

- If you are providing a product to your potential customers are you creating it or are you promoting an already made product?

With the information you have available you can write out your business plan. Don't get overwhelmed with this. When writing your business plan remember it doesn't have to be perfect so to speak. As your business grows and you have more ideas, you can add these ideas to your business plan. Try to be as detailed as possible, while leaving room to be able to make changes along the way.

A business plan consists of the following:

- Executive Summary—summary of your business idea and its direction.
- Company Description—description of the company, what are you offering, and what makes your business stand out.
- SWOT Analysis—strengths, weaknesses, opportunities, and threats for your business.
- Marketing Plan—how you plan on letting the market know about your business.
- Operations Plan
- Management Plan—Are you the owner and operator or you will hire a management team to assist you? Explain.
- Financial Plan—if you are borrowing money to open your boutique you have to express how much you need and what you plan to use the money for both short term and long term. This

portion also must include how you plan on paying the money back.

For more information about business plans and how to create a plan that works best for your business, you can visit sba.gov.

Boutique Notes

After reading this chapter, what were your aha moments?

_____
_____
_____
_____
_____
_____
_____
_____
_____
_____
_____
_____
_____
_____
_____
_____
_____
_____
_____
_____
_____
_____
_____
_____
_____
_____

Chapter 6

PRODUCT AND/OR SERVICE

You must know what type of product or service you want to provide. If you are not sure this is the perfect time to figure that out. Most boutiques sell items such as

- Women's clothes
- Men's clothes
- Children clothes
- Shoes
- Pocketbooks
- Jewelry
- Hair
- Health products
- Or a combination of these products

Services that can be offered are as follow:

- Marketing
- Branding

- Photography
- Website design
- Law services
- Financial services
- Credit repair services

Women

In deciding to open a women's clothing boutique you have many options. You can offer jeans, shirts, dresses, skirts, business wear, casual wear, evening wear, or a combination of them all. Based on the vision you have for your boutique you can decide which one works best for your business.

Men

Servicing men is different from servicing women because it is not an activity that men do often. Most men leave the shopping to women. When men do have to shop, they are focused on what it is they need. Offering products such as jeans/pants, shirts, business wear, formal wear, outerwear, underwear, and socks are some items you can start with. Offering specialty items for men who are big and/or tall is another area that you can specialize in as well.

Children

Children stores normally offer a wide variety of products. One must consider the age range of the child as well as any accessories they may want to offer. Consider whether you would like to have a children store that specializes in products for infants, toddlers, preschoolers, grade schoolers, or adolescent or a combination of them all.

Shoes

Online businesses that sell shoes or what we now call Shoetique for online shoe sellers is another great market. Women shoetiques are on the rise. You can also consider an online shoe business for men and children.

Pocketbooks/handbags

Normally handbags and pocketbooks are sold in stores that cater to women. If you have a unique design and something different you can bring to the market, put it out there. See what kind of feedback you get, and go from there.

Jewelry

Women love jewelry and accessories to complement their outfit. You can add this to your boutique that cater to women or establish a boutique just for people who love accessories just as much as you do!

Hair extensions

Hair extensions are a market that is very popular. Most hair stylist and salon owners carry their own line of hair extensions. Offer your hair extensions in your online boutique to generate additional income. Let your clients give testimonies of how the hair feels and how long it last. I will share with you some additional marketing methods later in this book.

Health products

Healthy is the new sexy! So many people are looking for health and wellness products to help them lose weight, feel great, and do it quickly. You can cater to men, women or both.

The service industry is expanding and online boutiques are popping up everywhere. These are just a few of the markets you can tap into.

Marketing

Facebook marketing, Instagram marketing, Twitter marketing, Internet marketing, Offline marketing, Attraction marketing is just some of the areas of expertise you can create an online business for.

Branding

Branding a business is major and can change the direction of the business quickly. If you specialize in helping business to make their brand bigger, you can provide services for them online that will do just that.

Photography

A picture is worth so much. Making sure to captures those moments create memories that will last a life time. If this is something you specialize in, showcase your work on your business page. Create a way for people to invest in your services online.

Website design

Having a website is like owning a piece of real estate. You want your house to look its best and function properly for years to come. Visitors will come over often so it must be welcoming right? This is what website designers do. If this is something you specialize in, you can develop service packages that allow people to do business with you.

Law services

A lawyer can specialize in many things. If you are a lawyer that specializes in business startup to assist entrepreneurs in forming the right business structure, you can advertise this on your website. Let people know what it is you specialize in and how they can invest in your services.

Financial services

Show people how to make their money work for them. If you provide a service that will help people get out of debt, save money for vacation, or even save for retirement, put a package together in these areas and provide it to people. Everyone could save a little money and services like this are always needed.

Credit repair services

Creditors look at your credit score to determine if you are going to have that car, house, or that loan you need to help pay for something. This is a big deal. People everywhere can use this service. Develop a package that will help people get the negative items off of their credit report and show them how to keep them off.

If you don't want to stick to a specific product or service you can think of a theme that you would like.

For example, Valentine day themes, party themes, or a family theme can be a great way to create a unique boutique idea. Valentine day is a romantic holiday that symbolizes love. Your boutique can have that type of appeal.

Party themes are popular as well. When I think party themes it reminds of the store Party City. You may have a unique party theme idea and want to expand it. Don't limit yourself or your ideas. Make sure you have a few products to start with. You can always add to your collection once you get up and running.

Boutique Notes

After reading this chapter, what were your aha moments?

_____

_____

_____

_____

_____

_____

_____

_____

_____

_____

_____

_____

_____

_____

_____

_____

_____

_____

_____

_____

_____

_____

_____

_____

Chapter 7

MARKET RESEARCH

Conducting market research will allow you to find out if your business model exist and give you some ideas as to how you could run your boutique. You can also find return policy, shipping information, privacy policy, as well as frequently asked questions (FAQ) when conducting market research.

Market research allows you to search the type of business you want to open to see

A. If it exist
B. Who is your competition
C. Who is interested in your product or service
D. If it will be profitable

When conducting research it is a great idea to use Google.com as they are ranked #1 in the world for the most visited site. If you don't believe me just go to alexa.com. An example of how to search is as follow:

Look up boutiques that are similar to what you will offer in your boutique on Google. Make sure to type in exactly what you are looking for in the search engine. If you are random your search results will not get you what you want. Check out the sites on the first few pages of Google. Use the website to compare prices, check out the products they are selling and the style, and if customers are giving them feedback. Feedback will allow you to see if customers love or hate that particular product. Don't get discouraged by the competition. This lets you know if your idea will work or if you need to tweak it. Use this time to see what the average price is for the product or services. Alexa.com will also tell you how many people look up that particular site as well.

If you see some of the competition on social media sites such as Instagram, check out how many followers they have and what hashtags they are using. This is a great indicator of how many people could potentially be interested in your product or service.

Let's just say you want to sell skateboards. You know that this is a product that already exists. What you do not know is how much you want to sell your skateboards for, and you are having a hard time figuring out how to get your product in front of the right people aka potential customers. To find out this information you need to perform a search. Start off by finding out how much skateboards are retailing for. You can find out using search engines such as

Google.com. Once you find out the average price of a skateboard you can determine the cost for yours.

Next, you will find out more about people who skateboard and where they hang out. What's the average age of a skateboarder? Where do they live? Do they work, go to school, or both? On average, how much do they make? Are they boys, girls, or both? Are they using social media? Your research should allow you to get clarity on your potential customers.

These questions are critical and need to be answered because when it is time for your prelaunch, you need to know where to find them so you can let them know about this amazing product that you have to offer them. If your potential customers are high school students, you have to make a decision as to what you want your price to be because most high school students don't have a job. If they are hanging out on social media you need to find out where so you can advertise in that area. If they are on Instagram you may not want to spend much time on Facebook or Pinterest.

I hope you understand why this is so important to your business. Without narrowing down who your customers are you will be marketing a product to people who are uninterested in your product which will lead to you not being able to help your potential customers.

Keep in mind, when doing your research you want to stay true to who you are. I realize that in doing research sometimes our mind will start to adapt the ways of the competition, and suddenly we find ourselves doing exactly what it is they are doing. Stop! Don't mimic everything they do. Your mission is to stay true to you and the vision that you have for your boutique. Your goal is to find what the customers need and service them in that area. Focus your attention on areas of your particular market that are underserved. Think about a shopping experience that you've had. What was it that could have been done to make you keep coming back for more? Whatever that is, treat your customers the way you want to be treated when you go into a store or visit that website.

Questions to answer are as follow:

1. Do you know if your product or service already exists?
2. If you are selling a product, is your product already on the market?
2. What company is offering this product and whom are they offering this product to?
3. Where do your potential customers live?
4. Do they work, go to school, or both?
5. On average, how much do they make?
6. Are they boys, girls, or both?
7. Are they using social media? If so, which ones?

Boutique Notes

After reading this chapter, what were your aha moments?

_____

_____

_____

_____

_____

_____

_____

_____

_____

_____

_____

_____

_____

_____

_____

_____

_____

_____

_____

_____

_____

_____

_____

Chapter 8

TARGET MARKET

Target market in a nutshell is defining your target customers' identity or the businesses that you believe will purchase your product or services. Is it a male or a female, how old are they, do they work, these are the questions you have to ask yourself to determine who your target market is.

Defining your target market will allow you to determine

- Whether there is enough demand for the product or service you want to offer
- Tweak your business idea to better meet the needs of the potential customers
- Tailor your product or service to meet the customers desire

- Target your marketing efforts to reach your most promising prospects
- Craft your marketing messages appropriately—tone, language, and attitude to appeal to your best prospects.

Defining your target market is a good thing. Don't feel like if you do this you will lose out on customers because you will not. It will allow you to target your audience so that you can specifically target the people you know will purchase your product or service.

Defining your target market will allow efficiency. Instead of spending money in markets where you are not sure if they are going to buy, you can use that time to market in areas where you know your market is. You define your target market by these characteristics:

A. Age
B. Gender
C. Income level
D. Buying habits
E. Occupation or industry
F. Marital status
G. Family status
H. Geographic location
I. Ethnic group
J. Hobbies and interest

Examples of this are as follow:

If you are selling pregnancy clothing you will want to target women that are 25-40 years old, pregnant women who are married, who work in a professional setting such as finance, state or local job, etc.

If you are selling hair extensions you would target 18-35 year old women, single and married, working professionals with an income of 25k to 50k annually who already where hair extensions.

If you are targeting businesses you want to look for the following:

A. The size of the industry
B. Number of employees
C. The amount of annual sales
D. Location

Knowing exactly who your customers are will allow you to cater to them as much as possible. Keep in mind that you are fulfilling a need and providing service to an underserved market. The more you know about them the better your service will be.

Boutique Notes

After reading this chapter, what were your aha moments?

_____

_____

_____

_____

_____

_____

_____

_____

_____

_____

_____

_____

_____

_____

_____

_____

_____

_____

_____

_____

_____

_____

_____

_____

_____

Chapter 9

WHOLESALE AND BEYOND

If you are offering a product you have to determine where you want to get that product from, or how you are going to create it. You have to determine if you are going to make the product yourself or if you are going to have a manufacture create this product for you. You can also look into wholesale and drop shipping as well.

Some online boutique owners make a lot of their items to sell. This would be considered manufacturing. Other times they may fine a designer who will design and make the items for them to sell in their boutique. You have to determine if this is a route you would like to take.

Another option is wholesale. You can purchase products at wholesale prices, have them shipped to your location and sell them once they arrive. You to make informed, educated decisions about your boutique! Also, when contacting wholesale providers please make sure you are very professional. The wholesaler must know that you are serious about doing business with them.

Drop shipping is another option as well. Drop shipping companies are the middleman between the manufacturer and the boutique owner. Once you find a drop shipper that sales what you are looking to provide to your customers, test them out. Some drop shippers have a bad reputation and you want to make sure that if you are going to work with them, they can deliver the orders on time to your potential customers. Some examples of drop shipping companies that provide women's clothing are BuyTrends and Sammy Dresses.

Showrooms are a great place to get some ideas as well. They have showrooms in different areas around the world. I will list some of them below. See which area is close to you and take some time to pay them a visit.

- The Fashion Center located in New York, NY fashioncenter.com
- Miami International Merchandise Mart Located in Miami, FL miamimerchandisemart.com

- Atlanta Apparel Mart located in Atlanta, GA
  americasmart.com
- Dallas Merchandise Mart located in Dallas, TX
  dallasmarketcenter.com
- Denver Merchandise Market located in Denver, CO.
  denvermart.com
- California Market Center located in Los Angeles, CA
  californiamarketcenter.com
- Montreal Fashion Mart located in Montreal, Canada
  montrealfashionmart.com

For a list of other wholesale providers and manufactures go to openanonlineboutique.com/wholesale-directory

The last option you have is to resale products. Secondhand items or vintage clothing stores are becoming very popular. Websites such as craigslist and eBay allow you to resale your used items.

Boutique Notes

After reading this chapter, what were your aha moments?

_____

_____

_____

_____

_____

_____

_____

_____

_____

_____

_____

_____

_____

_____

_____

_____

_____

_____

_____

_____

_____

_____

_____

_____

_____

Chapter 10

FUNDING YOUR ONLINE BOUTIQUE

Now that you know the basics to opening a boutique, you need to have the funds to do it. There are so many creative and traditional ways to raise the money needed to fund your boutique and I want to share some of them with you. I have learned about some of these creative ways to raise money because I was in this position myself. I wanted to open my clothing boutique and had everything I need except inventory. It wasn't expensive to form the business, get the tax ID number, and open the bank account. It cost nothing to set up accounts with the wholesale providers I wanted to conduct business with. I honestly just didn't have the money I wanted to start a boutique I felt was worth opening. I know you're supposed to start slow and then expand and that was my plan.

I knew I needed about $2,000.00. I didn't have it at the time and it turned my excitement into frustration. My frustration eventually turned into procrastination, and once I started to procrastinate it seems as if I mine as well not follow through with it. I am so happy that I didn't let my frustration set in and take over. I knew owning a boutique was something I wanted to do and once I got out of my feelings and activated my faith things started to turn around. You will get frustrated some times, but don't let that frustration turn into you not taking the necessary steps to open your boutique.

Having a startup budget will be very beneficial. Below is a list of expenses to start your online boutique:

- Inventory
- Marketing and advertising
- Branding
- Website design and hosting
- Domain name
- Permits and license (depending on location)
- An accountant/accounting software
- A lawyer

Ongoing cost for your boutique will be inventory, website maintenance, marketing and advertising. To help with funding your boutique here are some funding sources that can help you to open and grow your online boutique.

- **Family and Friends**—Starting with people you know and trust like family and friends is one of the resources you can use to start your boutique. Let them know what your vision is for your boutique and how much money you need to get things started. Let them know that you have a plan and a projected income you would like to make in the first three months. Letting them know when you will pay them back will increase your chances as well. Most people won't mind lending money but they do want some type of time frame as to when you will be paying them back.

- **Fund Raisers**—Do something that will raise money for your boutique. If you love to cook you can sell dinners on a Friday or Saturday. I have seen family members do this to raise money for weddings, family reunions, and even medical expenses. I have seen churches do this to raise money for a program or an outing that members wanted to attend but didn't have the funds at the time to participate. I have even seen cheerleading teams raise money by selling candy to go to Disney World when they won the state competition and needed money so the entire team can attend.

- **Create An Information Product**—some people are very knowledgably in certain topics. I have witness people create Ebooks, share it on social media with their entire network, sell it for $10, and people purchase it. If you get 30 people to purchase your $10 product that only cost you your time, you just made $300.

- **Sell Items You Don't Need**—I am not one to keep a lot of furniture in my house, but I do know people who do. My mom is always purchasing furniture and little statues to put inside of her wall unit, but when she downsized she couldn't bring everything with her. Having a yard sale or garage sell as some people call it would have been ideal for her. She could have got rid of a lot of the furniture and made money doing it. If you have anything in your house that you don't need such as furniture, electronics, clothes, shoes, books, think about selling them at a garage sell or even to the Salvation Army. People do things like this all the time. Use the money you received to help you open your boutique.

- **Make Something**—I know that most of you are very talented people. You can make something, sell it, and generate the startup income needed to open your boutique. I have an aunt who makes a delicious Sweet Potato Pie. When she made these pies for church functions, and family events, people started inquiring. She made a few pies for some people at no cost, but eventually she turned her talent and passion for cooking into a profitable business.   You may not like pies you may like cupcakes, bake them and sell them to friends, family, and people having events. I have another friend who knows how to crochet. She would make her daughter beautiful hats and scarves for the winter.   When her daughter went to school the teachers and parents admired the hats and wanted them for their children. My friend turned her talent into cash by making custom hats and scarfs for the teachers, parents, and students.

- **Join A Network Marketing Company**—I know you may be thinking how is this going to help me open a boutique.   Truth be told I leveraged a network marketing company to help me open my business. I was strategic about it and you must be too. Keep the reason why you are doing things at the forefront.   Get with a company that has products that are truly helping people and are in high demand. I starting with a health and wellness company. I knew I needed to lose some weight, I tried the products, they worked, I told my friends and family, they brought the products, I got paid a commission, they lost weight too, it was a win win for everybody. I used that money to get the things required to open my boutique. Honestly, it was as easy as it sounds. Get involved with a company that will not only benefit you, but benefit everyone. Who knows, you may even want to incorporate the health and wellness products into your boutique business. Having more than one stream of income is always a good thing!

- **Keep Your Day Job**—Allow you full time or part time job to fund your business ventures. When people are upset Monday morning about going to work I'm not. You know why, because I know that this job is helping me by providing the income I need to open my boutique. Every time I get paid I put a percentage of money to the side that is specifically for my boutique. When you set your goals use the things that you already have to create the income that you need. Don't quit your job because you feel like your boutique is going to make you a millionaire. While that may be true, the fact of the matter is that you are not a millionaire yet. Be strategic! Change your mind set about going to work. Once you set in your mind that this job is going to allow you to open your very own online boutique, you will get excited about going to work on Monday!
- **Government Programs**—there are government programs that will assist small business owners. Go to sba.gov and see what the requirements are to funding a new or existing business.

Boutique Notes

After reading this chapter, what were your aha moments?

_____

_____

_____

_____

_____

_____

_____

_____

_____

_____

_____

_____

_____

_____

_____

_____

_____

_____

_____

_____

_____

_____

_____

_____

_____

Chapter 11

NAMING YOUR ONLINE BOUTIQUE

Find a name that suits your boutique's vision as well as the product or service you are offering. Write a few names down that you think will be a great fit for your boutique. Step away for an hour and come back to it. Sometimes when you step away and come back to it your mindset is a little different. Names you thought of will get scratched off of the list slowly but surely until you come up with that one name that makes you smile, and brings you joy every time you say it and every time you see it on paper. When you get that name you need to make sure the domain name is available to purchase, register that name with your county clerk's office, set up an email account, and claim social media.

Purchase your domain name immediately. The domain is simply the address you put in when you are online and want to go to a particular site. For example, www.google.com is a domain name. Purchase your domain name from www.godaddy.com.

You don't want the name of your boutique to be "Dresses Are Us" and your domain name is "Dresses At Its Best.Com". You will confuse your potential customers and miss out on sales. Keep in mind customers don't want to be confused. You want to create an easy, simple shopping experience for them so that they can buy without any problems. When things are too complicated it discourages the potential customer and they will leave off of your site faster than you want them to.

Set up your email account. With this portion you have option. Depending on your vision you can choose a free email account or you can choose a paid email account. Free email accounts you can choose from are yahoo and Gmail. For example, your contact email address with a free account will be xxxxxxx@gmail.com. However, it is in your best interest to choose an email address that if professional. You can purchase an email account with the company you purchased your domain name with. With this option your email address can be info@xxxxxxx.com. Do you see the difference here? Take the time to decide which one you would prefer. Once you do that go ahead and set it up.

Claim your social media accounts. Go to all of the social media sites you will be using to promote your online boutique, and name them. Facebook, Twitter, Pinterest, YouTube, LinkedIn, Instagram, and Periscope, are just a few of the social media accounts you should create accounts for. This will benefit you once we get to the branding and marketing section.

Boutique Notes

After reading this chapter, what were your aha moments?

_____

_____

_____

_____

_____

_____

_____

_____

_____

_____

_____

_____

_____

_____

_____

_____

_____

_____

_____

_____

_____

_____

_____

_____

Chapter 12

BUSINESS REGISTRATION

Getting the name of your business registered with the county you live in is the next important step to making your boutique come to life. If you decide to open your boutique as a sole proprietor, you will need to go to the county clerk office or designated area to open a business in the city where your boutique will be located. They will be able to walk you through the necessary steps to register your business. If you plan on opening your boutique as a limited liability company, my best advice to you would be to get professional assistance. Sites like Legalzoom.com can assist you with forming the business structure of your choice.

Registering your business with the city or with the

state if you opening as an LLC is crucial. Regardless of the way you decided to form your boutique business, you must contact the state to get an EIN number or tax ID number. If you are a sole proprietor you can use your social security number, but I wouldn't recommend it.

Whenever you are in the business of selling items you must charge a sales tax. This sales tax goes to the state that you are conducting business in. If you don't register your business with the state you will not get the certificate of authority you need to collect taxes. You must also provide this information to the wholesale providers that you intend on doing business with. You cannot open your boutique without this; this is a critical step.

When opening a sole proprietorship you will have the option of using your social security number for tax purposes, or you can call the taxation department and ask them if you can have a tax id number also known as an EIN (employer identification number). If you are uncomfortable with your social security number being used they can issue you a tax ID number to use when you are conducting business for your boutique.

With your certificate of trade name (boutique name) and EIN, you can now open a bank account. Make sure you bring original copies of this information. If you don't bring it, the bank may not allow you to open an account.

Depending on where you live this information can

be slightly different. Make sure to follow up with your local business office.

Now that you have your boutique name and formed your business entity, you can set up your accounts with your wholesaler providers, manufacturers, and/or drop shipping companies. If you decided to go with a wholesale provider they will need your certificate of authority faxed over to them with your identification. Depending on the wholesale provider they may need more or less information. Make sure you know what they need so that you can send it off to them all at the same time. Not sending everything can delay your boutique grand opening.

Boutique Notes

After reading this chapter, what were your aha moments?

_____

_____

_____

_____

_____

_____

_____

_____

_____

_____

_____

_____

_____

_____

_____

_____

_____

_____

_____

_____

_____

_____

_____

_____

_____

_____

_____

_____

Chapter 13

WEBSITE NECESSITIES

When it is time to move forward with creating a website you will have a few options to choose from. Once you solidify a hosting company you can then work on designing your website. Payment processing needs to be determined as well. Will you accept major credit cards through PayPal or another provider? You can hire a web designer to do all of these things for you. Of course it will be a fee involved, or you can do some research on ecommerce sites that may have everything you need to run your business smoothly, and give it a professional look.

Payment Processing

What form of payment would you like to accept? You want to make it easy for customers to make a purchase. I would suggest credit cards and PayPal. PayPal is good for people that are uncomfortable giving out their credit card information online.

Set up your PayPal account by going to www.paypal.com. I have two separate PayPal accounts, one for my business and one for my personal use. I recommend you set it up this way just so that you can keep your business and your personal finances separate.

Self-Hosted Website

A web host is the company that will allow you to use there server space to host your website for a small fee. You can get a web host from the same site you purchased your domain name from. With this option you can host your boutique on your own server. WordPress is a content management system that you can use to host your boutique website. With this option you own your site, and can customize it however you like. You will however need plugins (a function that will allow you to tailor your site to meet you and your customer's needs) such as Woo Commerce to allow customers to make purchases from your boutique. You also have to provide security for your site as well. When customers are making purchases they want to make sure their information will not be stolen. You must search for plugins that will allow the shopping cart on your website to be secure at all times. Controlscan.com is one company that offers security for websites. Godaddy.com is another company that offers security for your website. If you decide to use Paypal, they have a security feature already set up within their site.

1. Examples of webhosting companies are as follow:
    a. Godaddy
    b. Host gator
    c. Bluehost
    d. 1and1.com

A self-hosted site has several benefits. Most people gravitate towards hosted sites because they are easy to set up, user friendly, and because they are inexperienced when it comes to setting up websites. However, with the right tools and resources self-hosted sites allow room for growth. Three benefits to self-hosting your own site are as follow:

• **You own and run your website without any restrictions**. You have freedom because you own your website and you can provide whatever product or service your heart desires. With hosted websites there can be many restrictions, and you do not own the site.

• **No monthly fee**. Hosted sights charge monthly fees depending on how many items you are selling.

More products, more money. This does not include the transaction fees that you are charged for your customers to use their credit card.

- **No competition**.   Amazon, Etsy and eBay are examples of marketplace sites. With marketplace sites a customer can go directly to your web page and purchase items, or they can search for the type of product they are looking for. Once they have their search results in the market place they will find your products as well as other similar products listed on the site.

Ecommerce Solutions

If you are looking for a solution that will give you webhosting, allow you to design your boutique, and offer payment processing you should go with an Ecommerce solution. With ecommerce websites you pay a monthly or yearly fee to use themes and templates, which will allow you to design your boutique, and the storage space you need for the products you would like to sell. Most ecommerce sites provide analytics that will help you to monitor your traffic sources. This is great because you want to know where the traffic is coming from. Once you know where the traffic is coming from, you can market to that audience and continue to draw them in to your boutique to purchase your products. This will also allow you to see how many visits you get to your site and compare it to how many people actually make a purchase. Some ecommerce sites to choose from are as follow:

- Shopify
- Bigcommerce
- Supadupa.me
- Big cartel
- Squarespace

Do your research on the option listed above and pick which solution works best for you!

As a boutique owner you want to make sure you stay focused on products/services and marketing, and less on being a web designer. If you have money in your budget set aside it may be best for you to hire a web designer to get the perfect look for your boutique. Make sure the web designer trains you on how to operate the website without them as well. You don't want to get stuck paying a monthly fee to the designer for the upkeep of your site. If you are like me, a do it yourself entrepreneur you can go handle this all by yourself. I have managed to create several websites that operate as blogs and ecommerce sites. Setting up the foundation for a website only takes a few hours if not less than that. For more information you can visit my website openanonlineboutique.com as I help aspiring and emerging boutique owners get their boutique's business up and running with ease.

Boutique Notes

After reading this chapter, what were your aha moments?

_____

_____

_____

_____

_____

_____

_____

_____

_____

_____

_____

_____

_____

_____

_____

_____

_____

_____

_____

_____

_____

_____

_____

_____

_____

_____

_____

Chapter 14

STORING INVENTORY, PACKAGING & SHIPPING

In opening an online boutique you must decide where your inventory will be stored. If you decided on drop shipping or you are providing a service then this may not necessarily be for you. I will say to you that if you plan to create a multimillion dollar brand for your boutique you want to consider having a product you can call your own. Every celebrity has their own product. Whether it is a book, an album, a shoe or sneaker, perfume or cologne, everybody that is somebody has their own product. You can write a book about what you specialize in. For example, you may own a children's boutique. What inspired you to open a children's boutique. Your story could be one that changes someone's life. Writing a book will get the information out there. Again, don't limit yourself to just one thing. Once your boutique in up and running, start creating additional streams of income.

Inventory

You should find a safe location in your home office or office outside of your home to store your inventory. You want to keep your inventory in a safe place that is cool and will not damage the items in any way. Your inventory is your investment. Remember on all investments, you want to get a return on your investment. Choose a location that you will be comfortable storing your inventory.

Packaging

Packaging and shipping is an important part of your business. People cannot physically come to your store to make a purchase so you have to deliver the products to them. It's probably the last thing you thought about in regard to your boutique, but it is one that must be addressed before your grand opening. You must decide how you are going to package your items, and which company you want to ship your items once they are packaged.

To find packaging for your products it depends on what you are selling. If you are selling clothes you can simply Google "packaging bags for clothing". You can also go to ebay.com, which is where I purchased my packaging bags. Depending on the size you are looking for they will give you several options. A tip that I can give you is to purchase some stickers that have your logo on it (We will discuss logos in the branding portion). You can place your logo sticker on the outside of the clear package to allow the customer to identify with your brand.

What do you want to include in your package? Of course you want to include the items that they have purchased, but you can also use this opportunity to include other products and services that you may offer. You can also include words or encouragement, or a small free gift that lets them know you appreciate them purchasing this product from your boutique.

Shipping

For shipping you can choose between United States Postal Service (USPS), UPS, or FedEx. Since this may be your first time starting an online boutique you want to start small. I would recommend starting off with USPS. You can use their Priority Mail option. This option delivers within 2-3 days and includes tracking information for you and your customers' convenience. This is a great option because this is not being weighed. You can go to your local USPS store and talk to the customer service representative to find out exactly how it works and make an informed decision as to what works best for you. Also, please keep up with all of the tracking numbers. While we would love for everyone to be honest, some people are not. People will say they did not receive their order when you have the tracking number and it states that it was delivered. Saving your tracking numbers will make life much easier for you when you are dealing with customers that are not always honest and hold up a standard.

Boutique Notes

After reading this chapter, what were your aha moments?

_____

_____

_____

_____

_____

_____

_____

_____

_____

_____

_____

_____

_____

_____

_____

_____

_____

_____

_____

_____

_____

_____

_____

_____

_____

_____

Chapter 15

CUSTOMER SERVICE

How are you going to provide exceptional customer service to your customers? Will you have an 800 number they can call between certain hours? Will you have an email address specifically for customer service questions? What is your boutique's return policy? Customer service is important to your business. You can have the best prices in the world, but if people cannot connect with you or when they do connect with you you're rude they will not do business with you again. Take this time to figure out your availability and store policy.

Depending on if you are running your boutique full time or part time you can set up customer service hours that are convenient for you. For example, some people have full time jobs. They use their boutique to generate additional income for themselves and their family. If you know you get off from work at 4:30pm you can setup to call back all of your customers between 5:30pm-8:00pm, and use this time so that they can call you as well. You can also establish weekend hours. If you don't work full time, then of course you are free to establish your working hours to receive calls and to make calls. Make sure to post this information on your website so that people can know what to expect. Connecting with customers allows you to build a professional relationship with them. Once they are comfortable with you, they will continue to support your business.

1. I have a Google voice phone number. I use this on all forms of marketing and advertising. If you don't have an office line or you don't want to give out your personal cellular phone number which I would not recommend, you should go over to www.google.com/voice to get a phone number you can use for your business.
2. You can also purchase an 800 number for your business by using www.800.com or www.grasshopper.com/800numbers

What is your privacy policy for your boutique? Do you have information regarding shipping on your site? What is your return policy? When you conducted your market research in chapter 7, you should have gathered this information. You can tweak that information to fit your standards for your boutique. Keep in mind; if you are using an ecommerce site they will have a privacy policy as well. Make sure that what you have in mind compliments what they provide on their site as well. If you decided to host your own website, create pages for this information. Have a separate page for privacy policy, a separate page for return policy, and a separate page regarding shipping information.

Boutique Notes

After reading this chapter, what were your aha moments?

_____

_____

_____

_____

_____

_____

_____

_____

_____

_____

_____

_____

_____

_____

_____

_____

_____

_____

_____

_____

_____

_____

_____

LEVEL 3

PRE-LAUNCH

Chapter 16

BRANDING & PRE GRAND OPENING

Branding

Your logo, website, packaging and material used to promote, should all scream what your brand is. Your brand separates you from the competition. Your brand lets customers know what to expect from the products and services that you are offering. Use this time to figure out what your brand for your business will be. I could break down the importance of branding myself, but I believe that Entrepreneur.com does a phenomenal job. Go to http://www.entrepreneur.com/article/77408 and read up on branding from the prospective of an entrepreneur.

If your desire is to build a multimillion dollar brand, you have to focus on the image of your boutique. When you think about multimillion dollar brands what do you see? Think about brands like Pepsi, Duncan Donuts, and makeup companies like Cover Girl Cosmetics. What do they all have in common? Celebrities! The all have celebrities attached to their brand.

I remember when Queen Latifah was the face for Cover Girl Cosmetics. During football season Duncan Donuts always attach a football player to their brand. I don't watch football as much I use to, but last time I did they had Eli Manning as their celebrity attachment. Pepsi, which is already a popular brand took things to another level when they attached Beyonce to their brand. I can even remember when Carol's Daughter built their brand. I had no idea this company exist or what they were about. What made me pay attention to this company were the celebrity attachments which at the time was Jada Pinket Smith. The Weave Shop is another small business that branded themselves with a celebrity. Basketball Wives Reality Star Jennifer Williams was there celebrity attachment. With this celebrity attachment The Weave Shop was able to go from one location to have several locations in different states around the US.

Go back to your vision and see what direction your boutique is heading in. Don't limit yourself or your boutique. Think outside of the box and get out of your comfort zone. It's not until you do that amazing things will begin to happen, but you must create the path for those things to happen. Brand your boutique business in a way that you will get the most attention possible. Remember to never associate with anything or anyone one that can give your brand a bad reputation. Always work with people that are the image you want your boutique to be associated with.

Testing Your Site

If you read this book from the first page until now and followed everything step by step, you are ready to test your site. Go to your online boutique and make a purchase. Determine if the experience was easy for you. Did you like the flow of things? How long did it take you to check out? Did you receive an email about your purchase? Does it let you know when you will be receiving your items? Does your inventory automatically update itself? These are some of the questions you need to ask yourself after you made a purchase from your boutique website. If your experience was not to your liking, go back and change those things so that the process can be smoother for you and your customers. Do not think that everything will be perfect the first time. If you wait for perfection you will never get started. Fix the minor problems and test it again. Run your test until you are comfortable with the outcome.

Boutique Notes

After reading this chapter, what were your aha moments?

_____

_____

_____

_____

_____

_____

_____

_____

_____

_____

_____

_____

_____

_____

_____

_____

_____

_____

_____

_____

_____

_____

_____

_____

_____

_____

_____

Chapter 17

MARKETING

Marketing is important to your business because it determines how long your business will last. Marketing is important in the startup stage of your business as well as the launch stage of your business. You can have the best online boutique in the world, if no one knows about your boutique how can they buy any of your products? Marketing is the action or business of promoting and selling your products or services. To make your marketing efforts count you should utilize services such as social media sites, pay-per-click ads, email marketing, offline marketing and invest in a blogging platform.

There are several different ways for you to market you product or service.

Social Media

Social media is a free way to spread the word fast about the product or service you are offering. Facebook, Twitter, YouTube, Google+, Pinterest, Periscope, and Instagram, are some of the popular social media sites. These sites have millions of people registered to them, which mean you have access to this amount of people also. Getting your product or service in front of them can make a world of a difference for your business.

A. Facebook—Set up your business page on Facebook. Post different topics related to your boutique for customer engagement. Get your followers participation by asking them to share what they love about your products or services. Schedule your post by using the new feature that Facebook has for the business pages. It allows you to schedule post, which will save you time.

B. Twitter—Set up your twitter account for your boutique. Use Twitter to talk about any products or sale items you may have for the week. Send out tips that will be able to help customers with a product or service they purchased already. Make sure to follow customers and others with a large following and influence in your industry.

C. LinkedIn—create your LinkedIn profile and make sure that your profile is current with correct website links for your boutique and contact information. Depending on the products or services you are offering you can list them in your profile as well so that they can be visible to the people in your network. Make sure to join groups that are popular to your customers. Offer your input by answering any questions they may have, and even post a few questions on your own to see what problems people are having in hopes that you can provide them with a solution to the problem.

D. Google+ - Create a Google+ profile and create circles for different areas of your boutique. Customers would be an example of a circle you would create for your Google+ account. You can also start a Google+ community on topics that are related to your business. Hangouts which is a video chat tool created by Google is another great feature that you can use to bring awareness to your boutique and the products you are offering.

E. Pinterest—Set up a Pinterest profile for your boutique and create different boards that are relevant for your industry. Make sure to add the Pin It button to your boutique website pages so that visitors can post the image or pin the image from your Pinterest account. Pinterest also allows you to post videos. Make sure that you take full advantage of this opportunity as well.

F. Periscope—Periscope is a new social media tool that is exploding and is essential to your business. Set up a Periscope account, which can be connected to your twitter for your business page. I see so many people Periscope about their business and you should be too! Set up your Periscope account. Come up with ideas to discuss about your boutique products and/or services, and Periscope about them. Its new, it's a great leverage tool, and it's fun!

Promotions

Promotions are a great way to draw people to your website. You can offer weekly or monthly giveaways to potential customers for signing up for your email list. You can have contest as well, which is popular on social media sites such as Instagram. One thing I will say is to make sure you have a purpose behind your promotion. If you are looking to get more people on your email list, you can offer 10% off. Direct customers to your email list to get the code to use during check out time. This way you give the customer something, which is 10% off, and you get something, which is their email address to be able to communicate with them in the near future.

Video Marketing

Video marketing with sites like YouTube and the new Periscope—video marketing is very popular. You may be shy in front of the camera, but tapping into video marketing can bring visitors to your website. And the best part is that it's free! Start by creating a YouTube channel for your boutique. Add useful, resourceful, and fun videos that will encourage your customers to watch your videos and share them with their network. Contest is something else that is popular on YouTube. Create contest that will allow your customers to create videos about how they use your product or services. Share these videos with your network. It will boast your brand tremendously. Your Periscope videos that you create can be posted to your YouTube channel as well. Just make sure that you save the Periscope videos to your phone or tablet so that you can post them to YouTube.

Blogging

Blogging is critical to your online boutique business. Your blog should be your home base. Without a blog, where would people find you? Yes they can search Facebook, Instagram and all of the other social networking sites, but if those sites get shut down tomorrow where can your customers and potential customers go to find you? Everyone thought Myspace will last forever and while it is still being used, it's just not as popular as it used to be. Social media sites are for you to leverage your business, that's it! Having a blog will allow you to position yourself as the expert in your field. Your blog is where you would write your articles and post them. Your blog is where you would post your videos. Your blog is where people will come to get the free giveaways that you have. Your blog is the life line of your business.

Email marketing

Email marketing allows you to market your product or service to people that have opt in to you email list. Email marketing is essential because it allows you to have a line of communications to your customers at all times. It has been said to me several times from my coaches and mentors that if you are not building a list, you are not in business. When I say building a list, what I mean is that you have to have a system that allows you to collect email from your ideal customers. Offer them something in return for their email address. Do something for free, people love free stuff. You will be amazed as to how many emails you will get. Most importantly it allows you to build a relationship with them. When you offer your free giveaway you want people to opt in to your list. This is the purpose of a free giveaway. Your email list will allow you to share content from your blog. Creating an email list will allow you to:

a. Give them what they have asked for

b. Build lasting relationships with them
c. Track who is responding to your emails and who isn't.
d. Save money by sending emails instead of printed materials, or marketing in ways such as using television and radio.

Social bookmarking

Stumbleupon.com, delicious.com, digg.com, and reddit.com are some of the popular social bookmarking sites. Social bookmarking sites allow you to get more traffic to your website. Leverage these sites and track the progress.

Pay-per-click

PPC is a great way to get traffic when your site is new. PPC ads allow you to show up on the search engines for your keywords immediately, and they allow you to test different keywords to see which ones bring more customers to your website.

Offline marketing

Offline marketing is valuable as well. You don't want to get stuck in front of the computer all the time to where you don't know how to interact with people when your outside. I can honestly admit that, that is how I use to be. I am such an introvert and don't mind being that way, but when you are in business you have to learn how to get out and be social. How are people going to be exposed to your brand and everything that you have to offer if you don't tell them about it? You have to be strategic about everything you do in your business. Go to networking events and Meetups to connect with people that have similar businesses, and an entrepreneur mindset such as yours. I often go to Eventbrite.com and look up different events in my area to attend. Get business cards, flyers, and/or brochures to give to people you meet that are interested in knowing more about your boutique business. Go to seminars, conferences, and classes that will sharpen your skills in the industry you are a part of.

Boutique Notes

After reading this chapter, what were your aha moments?

_____

_____

_____

_____

_____

_____

_____

_____

_____

_____

_____

_____

_____

_____

_____

_____

_____

_____

_____

_____

_____

_____

_____

_____

LEVEL 4

LAUNCH

Chapter 18

ONLINE BOUTIQUE GRAND OPENING

Everything that has been discussed from living this boutique lifestyle, to mindset shifting, to boutique misconception, to products and service, to wholesale providers, ecommerce solutions, and marketing have led up to this point. It is time for you to launch your boutique business.

Now that you are aware of what is required to open your boutique, use this information to your advantage. Don't just sit on this information. I was in a class one day in Miami and my coach said something I will never forget. She told the class that she doesn't mind telling people what she does on a daily basis to get the results she is getting. She went on to say that only 10% of the people in the room were going to do exactly what she is saying. Everyone else will just know how to do it, but won't take the time to do it. Don't be that person. Don't get to the point where you have read this book in its entirety and you have not taken the steps to open your boutique. Do the research, find your target market, get your products, form your business, brand your boutique properly, set up your website, and launch! You don't have to be perfect to get started, but you have to get started to strive towards perfection.

A few months before your grand opening it would be beneficial for you to make people aware of your online boutique. Let them know that you will be opening for business soon by choosing a few of the social media platforms to market your boutique business. Show case what it is you are offering. Get people excited about your products or services to the point that they cannot wait for you to open for business.

By using social media you can also share behind the scene photos and videos leading up to the grand opening of your boutique. Fun photo shoots, pictures of inventory arriving from the post office, and pictures of you and your team working hard in preparation for your grand opening are ways to gain exposure to your boutique, and what products or services you are going to offer.

Make sure that you are leveraging networking events as well. Tell people what it is that you do and how they can get in contact with you by providing them with a business card. A technique I use when I want to connect with someone regarding business is to offer them some help. Let them know that you are more than happy to assist them and share with them how you are qualified to help them. That act of kindness can result in a business relationship that connects you to other entrepreneurs who are paying customers of yours.

Find out who is hosting an event and become a vendor. This is another way for you to get face to face with potential customers and show them what you have to offer. If you are in the clothing industry you can also put together a fashion show that will showcase your products to potential customers. Plan this event around the grand opening of your boutique and you will be surprised as to how much attention you will receive. An event like this will have to be planned and promoted properly, so make sure to give yourself more than a month to plan.

Whether you are promoting products or services, getting people excited about what you are offering will benefit your business. Think about it like this. When you are sitting down watching television and they show previews from a show that has not aired yet. They show you all of the juicy scenes from the upcoming show that make you want to tune in when it airs. That is what you want to do before the launch of your business.

Boutique Notes

After reading this chapter, what were your aha moments?

_____

_____

_____

_____

_____

_____

_____

_____

_____

_____

_____

_____

_____

_____

_____

_____

_____

_____

_____

_____

_____

_____

_____

_____

_____

_____

_____

Chapter 19

TIMING IS EVERYTHING

The first time I heard the phase timing is everything it was when a network marketer was trying to get me to join their business. While timing is everything in most companies that is not as important as the timing I am referring to. The timing I am referring to is the time you use throughout the day. You know, the same 24 hours in a day that everybody else gets. Your timing is everything personally and professionally and you have to have control over that before you can start something as serious as running a business.

A mentor once told me that if I don't manage my time, life would manage it for me. I thought about that for a while because I didn't understand it. I realize what my mentor was saying one day last year when I was just sitting at home reflecting on life and why I was not where I felt I should be. I realized at that moment I was just letting time go by and not taking advantage of it. I realized in that moment that there was so many things I could have done to get me closer to where I felt I should be in life, but because I was so relaxed with my goals and life in general I let time get away from me.

I wanted to share this with you because I want you to realize that your time is important. Time is more important than money. You can always make more money if you lose it, but once time is lost you can never replace it. You can never replace the time you didn't spend with your spouse. You can never replace the time you didn't spend with your children. You can never replace the time you didn't spend with your parents. You can never replace the time you didn't spend with your friends. You can never replace the time you didn't spend with you. You can never replace the time you didn't spend with God. People notice and always remember when you didn't set aside time to spend with them and do things that were important to them. You will start to remember the times you should have taken for yourself to clear and relax your mind. When you open your boutique and you realized it is not running as smooth as it should, you will realize that it could very well be because you didn't set aside the time to get you business affairs in order.

Timing is truly everything. This is why you have to create a schedule so that you can manage your time effectively. I recommend you use your journal as well as an 8 ½ by 11 weekly calendar. This is what I use to manage my time and make sure that the things I set out to do are getting done. If they are not getting done I evaluate what I did on that date to see where I may have wasted to much time. That way, you will be conscious of the time you spend doing certain things throughout the day.

Everyone is well aware that there are 24 hours in one day. For 7 days we have a total of 168 hours. The way most people use their time during the week is as follow:

- 56 hours for sleep
- 40 hours for work
- 42 hours for commuting, eating, family time, etc.

This is a total of 138 hours, which means we have 30 hours left in the week to be able to do other things. If you took 3 hours a day to work on your business, that is 21 hours a week. This means you have a little over an hour each day to pray, spend time with children, whatever it is that you desire to do. Even if you map out your schedule and you determine you can only spend 2 hours a day working on your business, that's 14 hours a week you are committing to your business.

This is a good start!

I wanted to show you this time table because I believe that we as people are not aware of how much time we spend on things that may not matter. I do want to be clear on one thing, don't neglect to spend time with your family to work on your business. This is a NO NO! You may be opening your boutique to provide for your family, but if you are neglecting spending time with your family to run your business they will start to resent you for it. I can only tell you what I know because I have experienced it.

When my daughter was about 2 months old I went back to work both a full time and part time job and I went back to school part time. I use to always drop my daughter off at her grandmother house because she used to take care of her for me while I went to work. Month would go by and I realized that I would only see my daughter late at night when I was picking her up, and early in the morning when I was getting her dressed and dropping her off again. I went to my daughter's grandmother house to pick her up because I happened to get off early, and when I walked through the door my baby was in the house, walking around in the living room crying and calling my name. This moment broke my heart for so many reasons. Number one, I didn't even know my baby was walking as well as she was. Number two, she was calling my name so clear and I never heard her call me like that before. Number 3, I realized that with all my working and going to school I truly missed some of the best years of my daughter's life. I took my baby home and as soon as I got in the house I held her so tight. With tears rolling down my face I just kept apologizing to my one year old. I apologize for not always being there; missing some of the important parts of her youth, and just letting life consume me. I felt horrible and I don't want this to happen to you. Do you have to make the extra money to support your family, yes! Don't neglect your family in the process because it will do more harm than good.

What I normally do is set aside time in the morning by waking up two hours earlier than I normally would. I also dedicate my lunchtime to my business 3 days out of the week, and I set aside an hour before I go to bed to work on my business. You have to do what works for you.

Timing is everything! Use your calendar and your journal to map out the times that work best for you & your lifestyle. Whether you work full time, part time, stay at home mom, or a student, you can run a business and it can be successful. Get rid of time wasters and rededicate your time to what really matters. Once you do this you will start to see a positive change and will be empowered to continue and will be more consistent in every area of your life.

Boutique Notes

After reading this chapter, what were your aha moments?

_____

_____

_____

_____

_____

_____

_____

_____

_____

_____

_____

_____

_____

_____

_____

_____

_____

_____

_____

_____

_____

_____

_____

_____

CHAPTER 20

ONLINE BOUTIQUE S.U.C.C.E.S.S.

What does it truly mean to be successful? Is it to accomplish all of your goals and dreams? Is it to make a lot of money? Is it for you to get married and buy the house with the white picket fence around it? Does being successful in your life involve other people? What does being successful truly mean to you? I personally feel like the word success is used so much and in my opinion it is overrated. Yes, overrated! I say this because when most people talk about success it is always filed with personal goals and accomplishments. I learned from being in the network marketing industry that you are not successful unless you help others to accomplish their goals and dreams. Success when you truly think about it is all about self, significance however is about helping others.

Because significance is not a popular word I decided to use the word success and create an acronym for it. I am not trying to encourage you not to have personal goals. You must have personal goals because you always want to evolve into a better person. Ultimately you becoming the best that you can be positions you to help someone else be the best they can be, which is where significance comes into play. When you really think about it every one that is great at something had someone there helping them to evolve. When you think of football players, basketball players, and sports in general, they have coaches that help them. Michael Jordan was good but he needed a coach. Eli Manning is good but he need a coach. Serena Williams is good but she needs a coach. Do you see the pattern here? You can be very talented at what it is you do, but to be a success in your personal goals you need a coach. Once you become the success, you pour into someone else who was once where you were and that's when you become significant.

I want to break down the word S.U.C.C.E.S.S. to you. I want to do this because it will help you to not just be successful when you open your boutique, but it will also help you to maintain it. Once this is broken down, you will realize that this may have started out as a personal goal, but in order to be a business owner you have to keep the needs of your customers in mind at all time. When my coach shared this with me it truly blessed me, and I know it wil do the same for you.

Secrets To Online Boutique S.U.C.C.E.S.S.

S eek to serve

- You must have a heart that wants to serve others when it comes to your online boutique business. It may have started off being about you, but once you decide to be in business it is about the customers.

U nderstand the needs of your customers

- You have to determine what are your customers' biggest needs? What problems are the facing? How could the work that you do for them improve their lives? What can you offer them that will make life easier for them?

C onnect with them through their desires

- Find out what it is that your customers' needs or desires to have. This can sometimes be found because it is some type of pain they have experienced. When you connect with people through their pains it creates the way for you to find a way to help them fulfill their hearts desires.

C reate a solution for their problems

- Most people are rich because they have created a solution to most people problems. If you watch infomercials you will see how it starts off with a problem that most people have. The creator of the product created a tool that would help to solve their problems. That is what you have to do. You have to seek to solve people problems. You find out their problems by asking what challenges they are having. Then you ask yourself how you can create the solution for their problems.

E xceed their expectations

- Depending on the type of boutique you plan to open you have to exceed your customers' expectations. You need to give them the WOW factor. Ask yourself what extra things can I create and provide for my customers that will allow me to go above and beyond their expectations? What would make them feel like I took care of them and that they can come to me if they ever need help in this area?

S eek to be a master in your craft

- Always remain a student and continue to educate yourself in the area of business you are in. Stay plugged in to what's going on in your industry and with your customers. Go to classes, seminars, conventions, and networking event that will allow you to be the best at what it is you do.

S ell your solutions by telling a story

- If you are a new business owner your audience may not know who you are. Share your story with people. You may not realize it but story telling is how people connect with you. Look at music artist as an example. Their songs are telling a story. When they have interviews and you find out that those songs are reflections of their life, it that same story is something you experience then you will relate to them. Once you can relate to them you feel like you know them and you build off of that. When it comes to your boutique you have to share your story so people can relate to you. Share stories like how you got started in the business. Share what it is like to be you for a day. Share what challenges, struggles, and frustrations inspired you to start your business. Share stories about your product or service. Share the stories of customers' who used your products. Testimonials from others especially emotional ones will help people see how you product or service worked for them and it will have a lasting effect on them.

If you want to achieve true success in your business you have to follow the 7 principles of success: Seek to serve, Understand the needs of your customers, connect with them through their desires, create a solution to their problems, exceed their expectations, seek to master your craft, and sell your solutions with storytelling.   Once you implement these principles into your business you will begin to see success and significance in your personal and professional life.

Boutique Notes

After reading this chapter, what were your aha moments?

_____

_____

_____

_____

_____

_____

_____

_____

_____

_____

_____

_____

_____

_____

_____

_____

_____

_____

_____

_____

_____

_____

_____

_____

Margin Notes

144

Chapter 21

YOUR MAP - MASSIVE ACTION PLAN

1. ***Choose This Day To Decide Exact What It Is You Want To Do***. Whether it is make more money, take more vacations, be debt free, further your education, provide a need to an underserved market, make a decision! Making a decision is the first step toward success and significance.

2. ***Write The Vision And Make It Plain***. Just like a map tells us where to go, you need your written map telling you where to go. Without a map you are going nowhere fast! Don't neglect this step; it is essential to your success.

3. ***Set A Reasonable Target Date For Your Goal.*** Your goals and the things that you want to accomplish are not unrealistic. However, the timing in which you set to achieve these goals may very well be. Make sure you set reasonable target dates as this will help you to reach your goals faster.

Don't get to relaxed and push the date far off, challenge yourself!

4. ***Write Down A List Of Ideas That Will Help You To Accomplish Your Goals.*** Let's say your goal was to lose 50 pounds within in a year. You know that cutting out fast food, exercising, and eating more fruit and vegetables will help you achieve these results. Write these things down. Get a yearly calendar in front of you and look at it. Calculate how many pounds you have to lose a month in order to achieve your goal of losing 50 pounds within a year. Fifty pounds divided by 12 month in a year is four pounds a month (50/12= 4.2 pounds). You can break this down even more because you know there are 4 weeks in a month. You know if you lose 1 pound a week you will achieve your goal of losing 50 pounds in a year!

5. ***Organize Your List.*** Now that you have your list you want to organize it by listing them in sequential order. Once you list your activities in sequential order you want to list them by priority. By doing this you know what needs to be done first to move you forward in the direction of accomplishing your goals for your boutique.

6. ***Take Massive Action!*** You know what needs to be done, you know the order in which they need to be done, get started! In order to be successful as a boutique owner you have to make the first step! You can wish, vision, write, plan, and plan some

more, but if you don't get up and do the work nothing will happen. Take massive action on your plans for your boutique today!!!

7. ***Be Consistent!*** Do something every single day that will help you to achieve your goals. Even when you dedicate a day for family, get up early in the morning before everyone else and do one thing that will move you in the right direction towards accomplishing your goals.

Boutique Notes

After reading this chapter, what were your aha moments?

_____

_____

_____

_____

_____

_____

_____

_____

_____

_____

_____

_____

_____

_____

_____

_____

_____

_____

_____

_____

_____

_____

Boutique Notes

After reading this chapter, what were your aha moments?

_____

_____

_____

_____

_____

_____

_____

_____

_____

_____

_____

_____

_____

_____

_____

_____

_____

_____

_____

_____

_____

Wholesale and Manufacturer List

Take the next step in your online boutique business by adding the Wholesale Directory List to your collection. The Wholesale Directory List includes over 40 wholesale distributors and manufacturers that offer products such as clothing, shoes, accessories, health and wellness products, beauty products, electronics, and more. Get the products you need to offer your customers today!

Also on OpenAnOnlineBoutique.com

- Free downloadable resources and worksheets that will help you get your online boutique up and running with confidence.
- Share *Secrets To Online Boutique Success* with family and friends. Discounted pricing is available for bulk orders of this book.

To have Shakeema speak to your organization about the principles found in *Secrets To Online Boutique Success*, email booking@openanonlineboutique.com

For more information about Shakeema visit www.ShakeemaHughes.com. Connect with Shakeema and a community of like-minded individuals online:

www.facebook.com/openanonlineboutique

www.twitter.com/openmyboutique

www.instagram.com/openanonlineboutique

Get FREE Access to Open An Online Boutique Resources!

Text **OAOB** to 313131. Once confirmed, in the body of the message type your email address and hit send. You'll receive free resources directly from Shakeema to support the success of your online boutique.

CPSIA information can be obtained
at www.ICGtesting.com
Printed in the USA
LVHW01s0401261217
560807LV00040B/3370/P

9 781517 736408